EASY PIANO COLLECTION
UPDATED EDITION

Disney/Pixar elements © 2019 Disney/Pixar

ISBN 978-1-5400-6464-6

Visit Hal Leonard Online at
www.halleonard.com

Contact us:
Hal Leonard
7777 West Bluemound Road
Milwaukee, WI 53213
Email: info@halleonard.com

In Europe, contact:
Hal Leonard Europe Limited
42 Wigmore Street
Marylebone, London, W1U 2RN
Email: info@halleonardeurope.com

In Australia, contact:
Hal Leonard Australia Pty. Ltd.
4 Lentara Court
Cheltenham, Victoria, 3192 Australia
Email: info@halleonard.com.au

I WILL GO SAILING NO MORE

from TOY STORY

Music and Lyrics by
RANDY NEWMAN

Brisk Fanfare

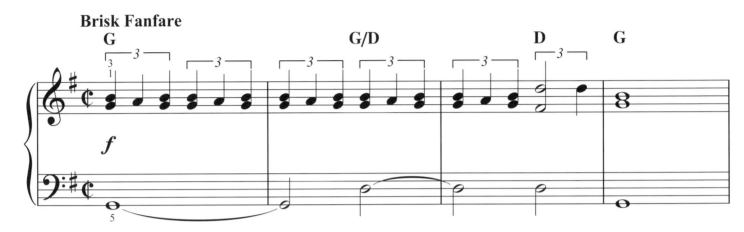

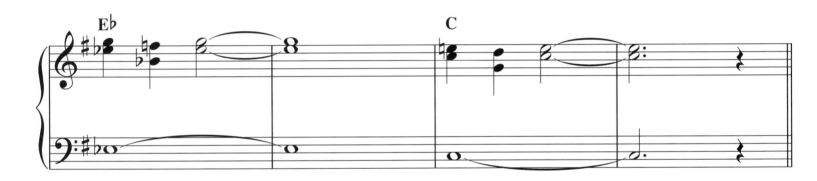

Slowly

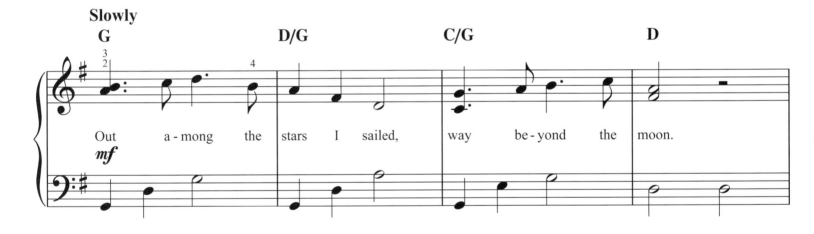

Out a-mong the stars I sailed, way be-yond the moon.

In my sil-ver ship I sailed in a dream that end-ed too soon.

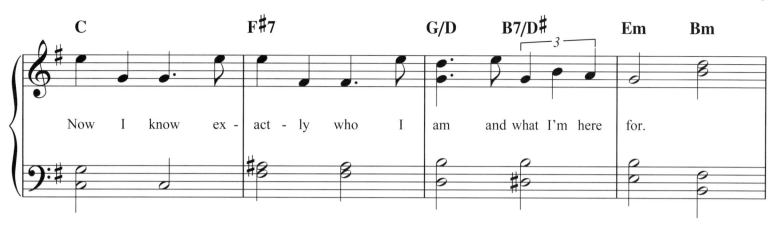

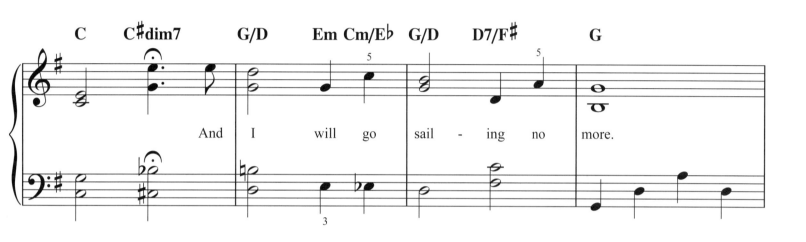

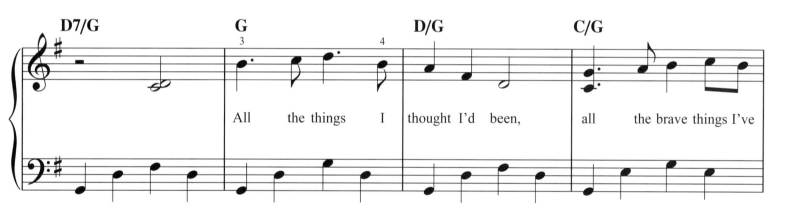

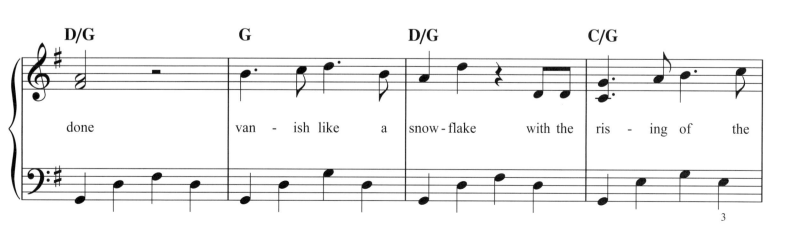

sun. Nev - er - more to sail my ship where no man has gone be -

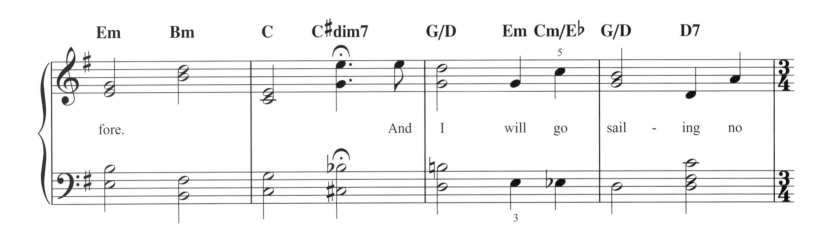

fore. And I will go sail - ing no

With motion

more. But no! ___ It can't be true! I could fly if I

want - ed to. Like a bird in the sky, if I be - lieved I could fly, why I'd

rit.

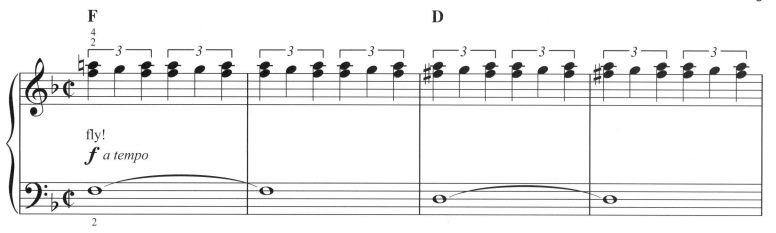

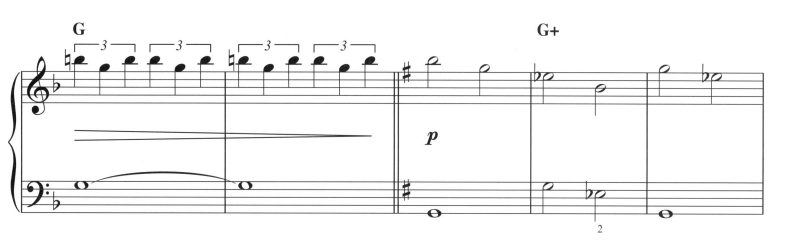

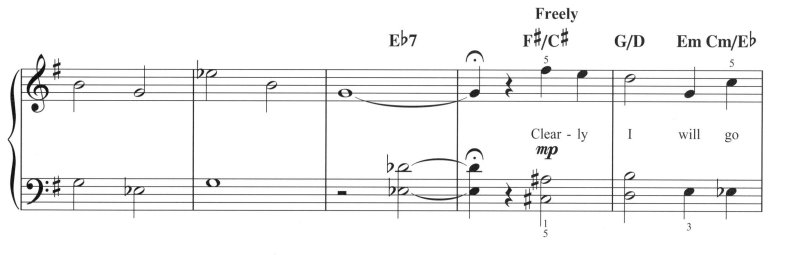

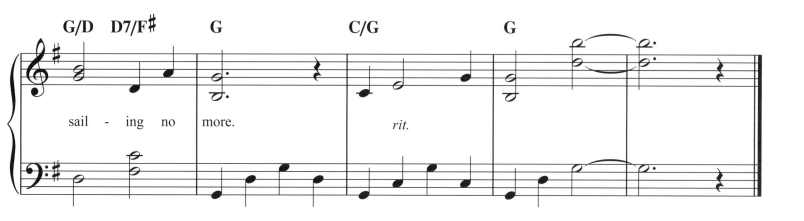

STRANGE THINGS

from TOY STORY

Music and Lyrics by
RANDY NEWMAN

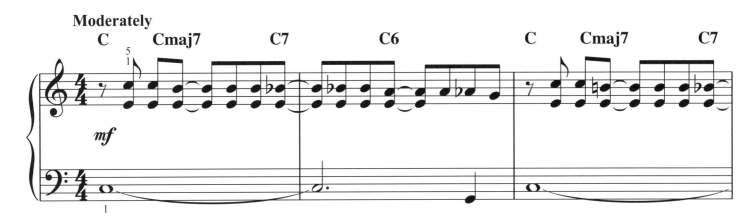

I was on top of the world, __ liv-ing high. It was right in my

pock - et.   I was liv-ing the life, __ things were

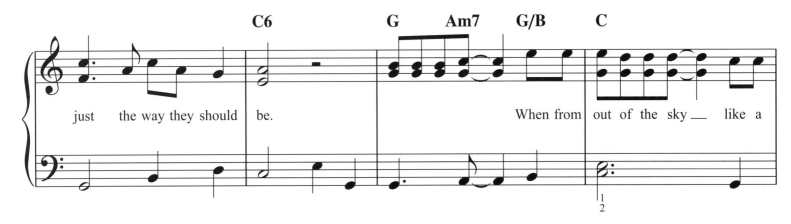

just the way they should be.   When from out of the sky __ like a

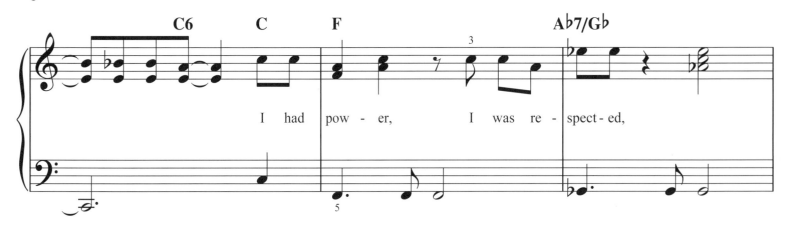

I had pow - er, I was re - spect - ed,

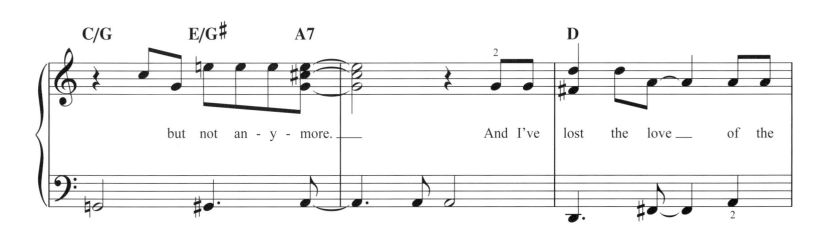

but not an - y - more. And I've lost the love of the

one whom I a - dore. Let me tell you 'bout it. Strange

things are hap - p'ning to me. Strange

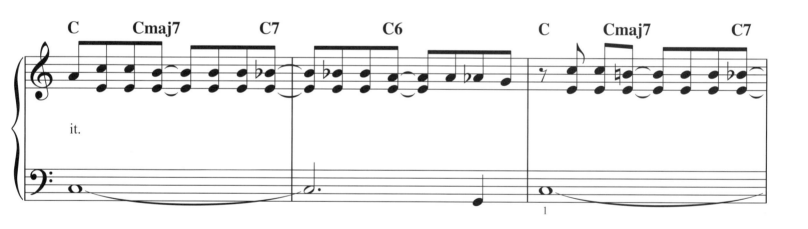

strang - er.   The min - ute you turn ___ your back,

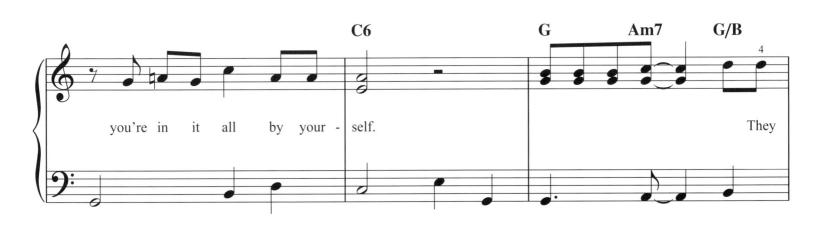

you're in it all by your - self.   They

laugh at your jokes, ___ you think you're do - ing quite well, but you're in dan - ger, boy. ___

And you end up a - lone and for - got - ten way up ___ on the

shelf. ___   Strange _____ things are

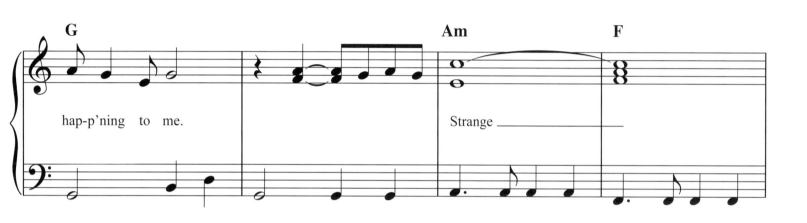

hap-p'ning to me.   Strange _____

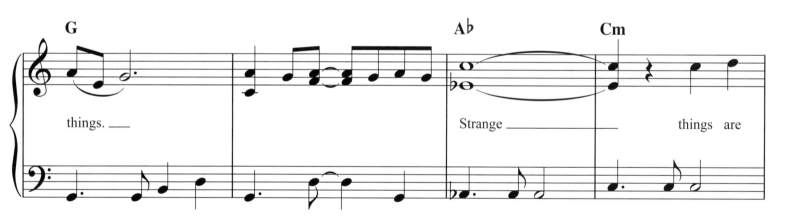

things. ___   Strange _____ things are

hap-p'ning to me.   Ain't no doubt a - bout __ it.

YOU'VE GOT A FRIEND IN ME

from TOY STORY

Music and Lyrics by
RANDY NEWMAN

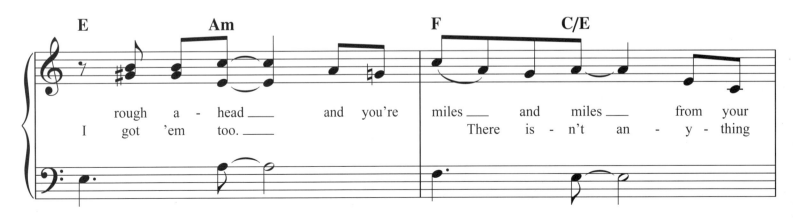

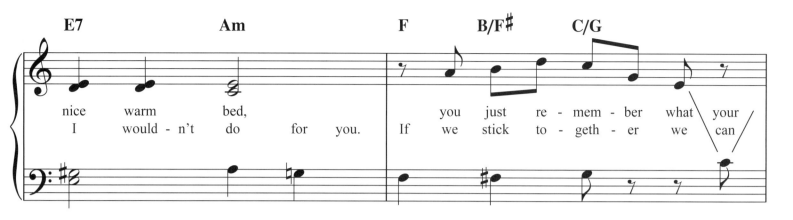

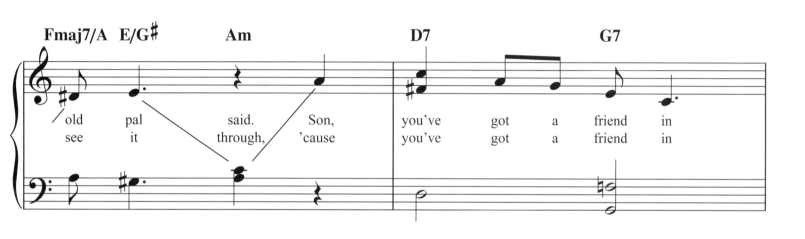

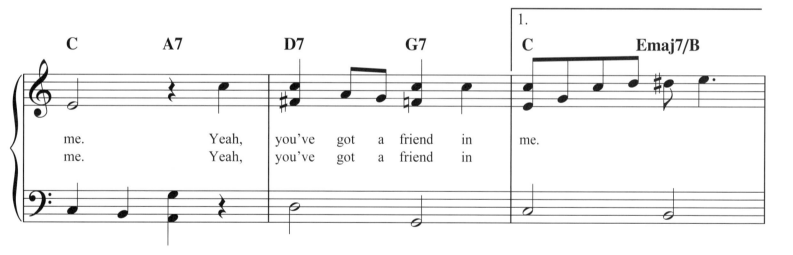

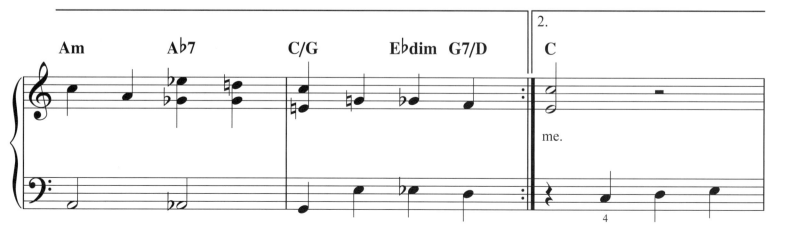

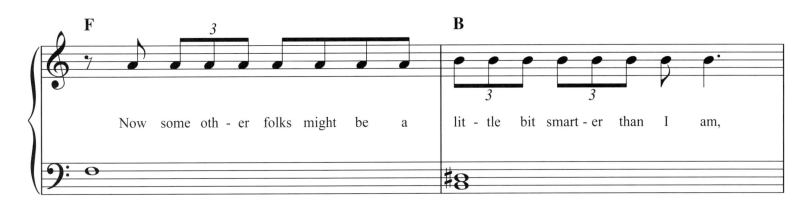

Now some oth - er folks might be a   lit - tle bit smart - er than I am,

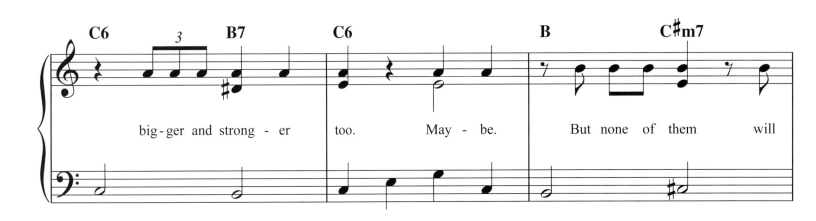

big - ger and strong - er   too.   May - be.   But none of them will

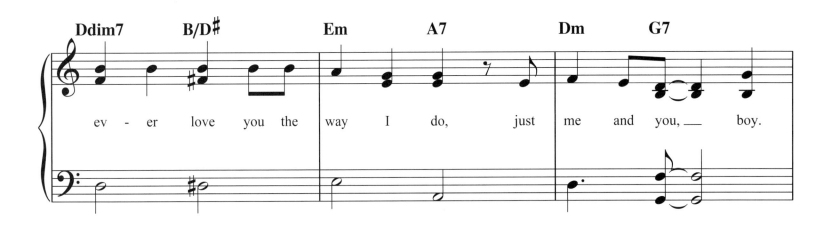

ev - er love you the   way I do,   just   me and you, ___ boy.

And as the years go   by,   our   friend-ship will nev - er

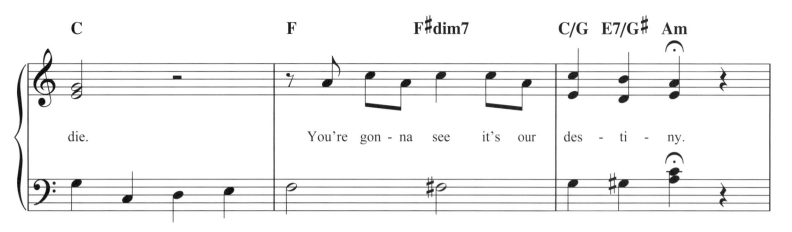

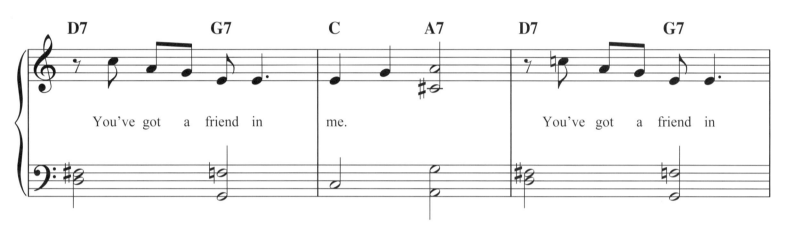

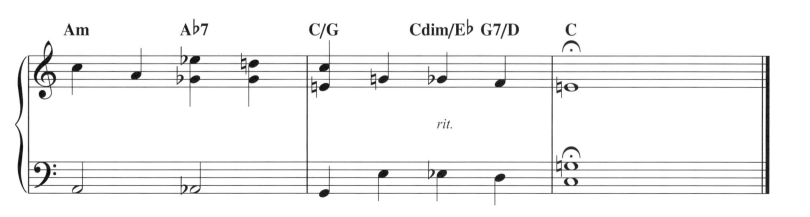

WHEN SHE LOVED ME
from TOY STORY 2

Music and Lyrics by
RANDY NEWMAN

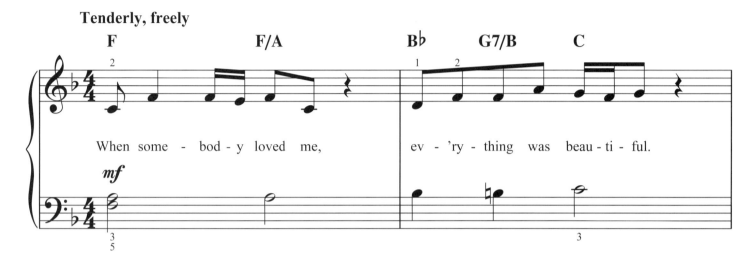

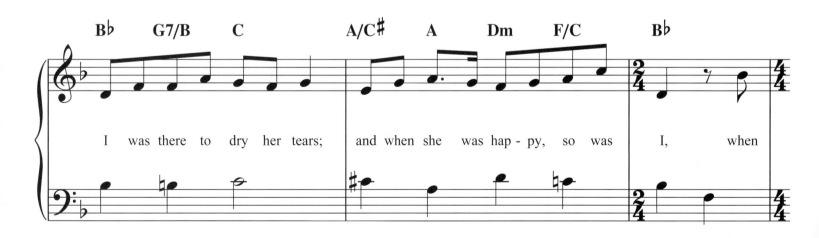

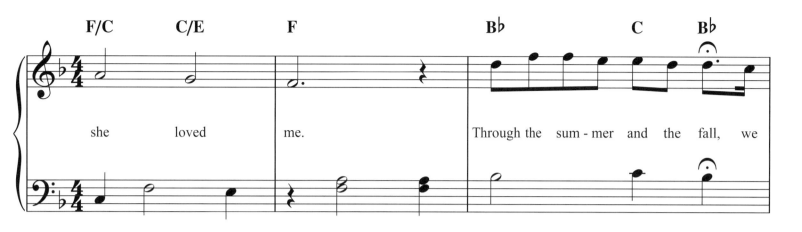

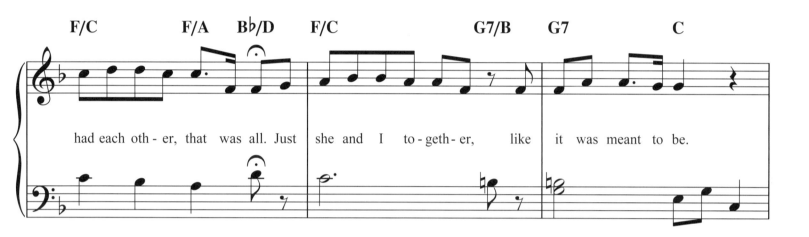

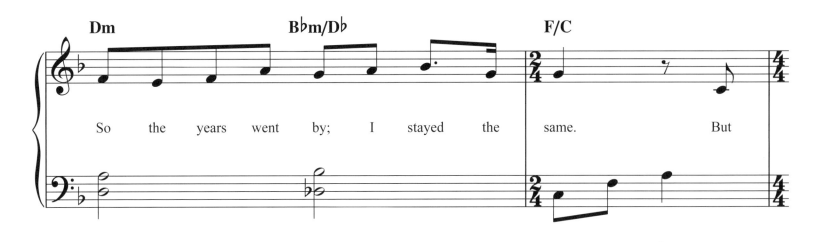

So the years went by; I stayed the same. But

she be - gan to drift a - way; I was left a - lone.

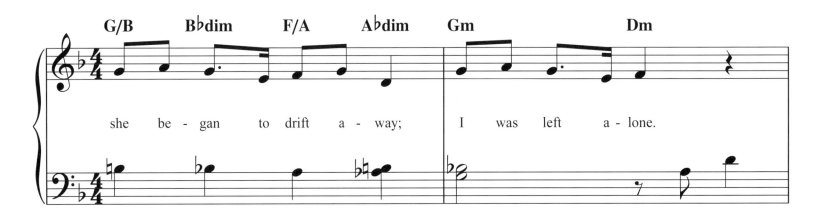

Still I wait - ed for the day when she'd say, "I will al - ways

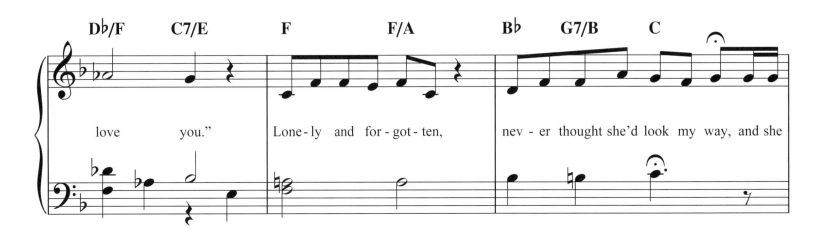

love you." Lone - ly and for - got - ten, nev - er thought she'd look my way, and she

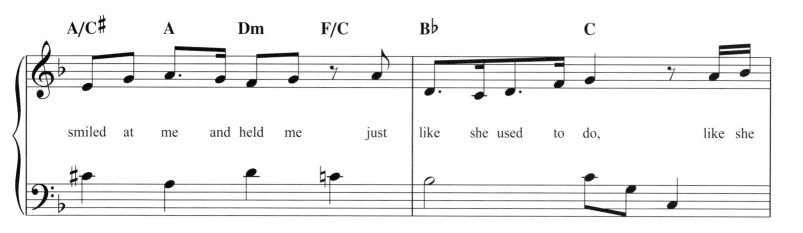

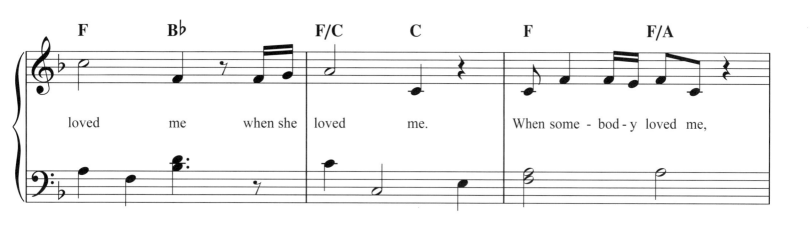

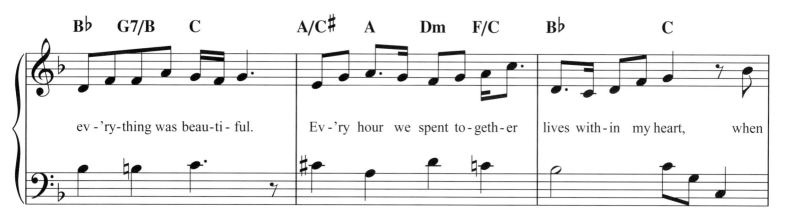

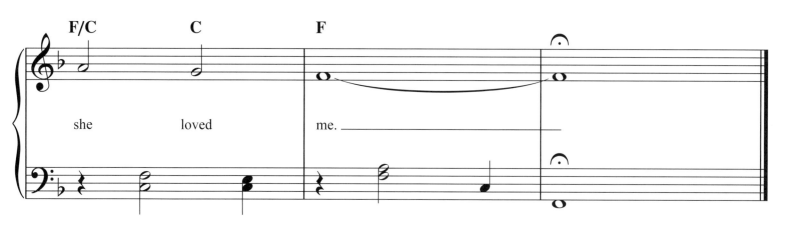

WOODY'S ROUNDUP
from TOY STORY 2

Music and Lyrics by
RANDY NEWMAN

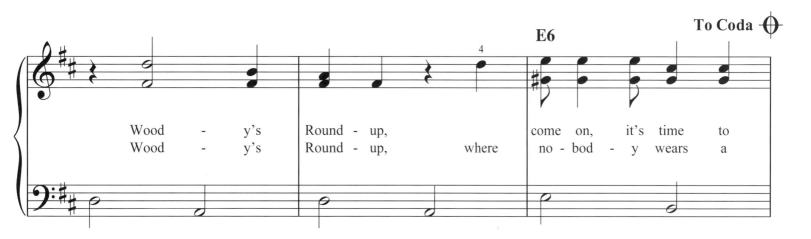

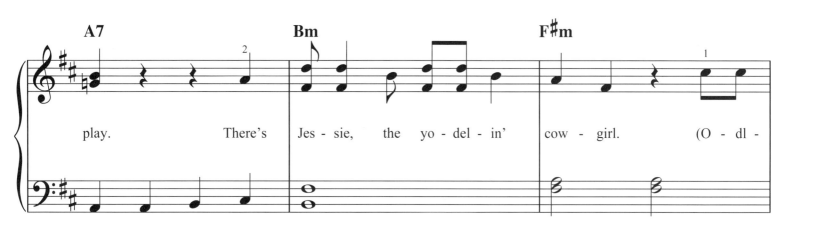

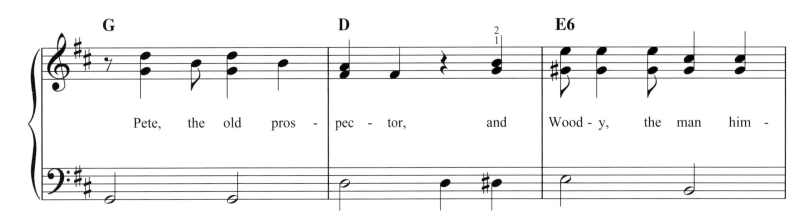

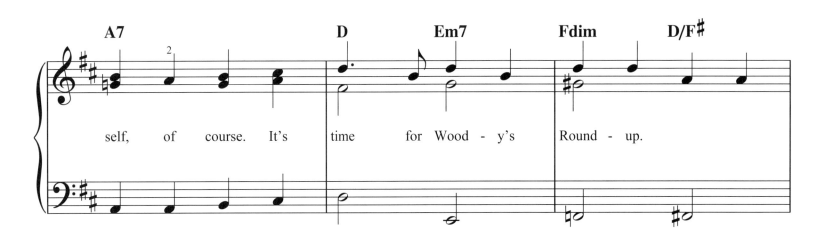

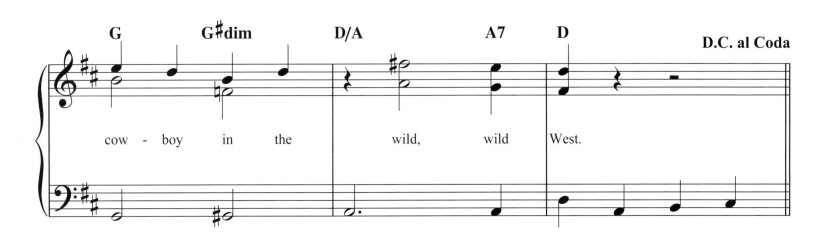

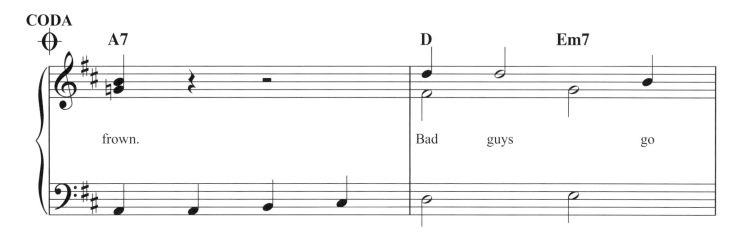

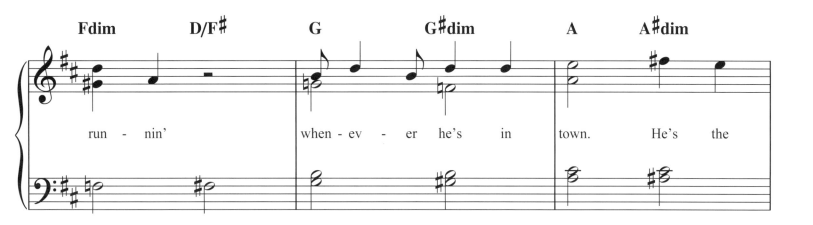

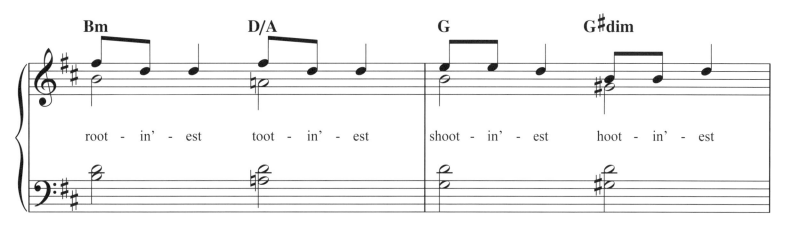

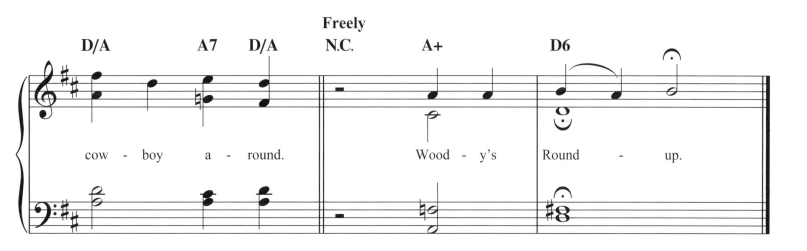

DREAM WEAVER

from TOY STORY 3

Words and Music by
GARY WRIGHT

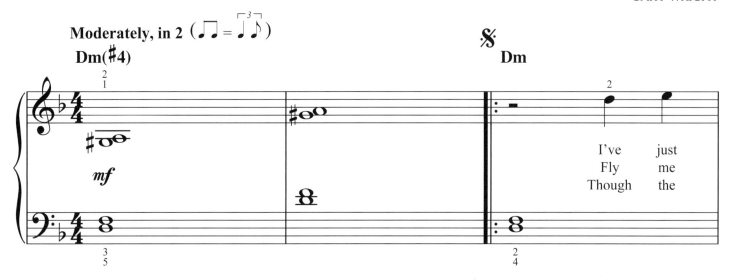

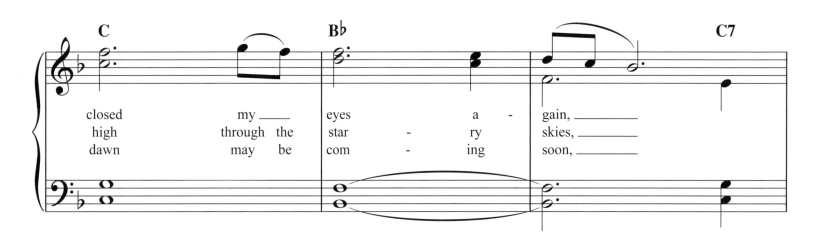

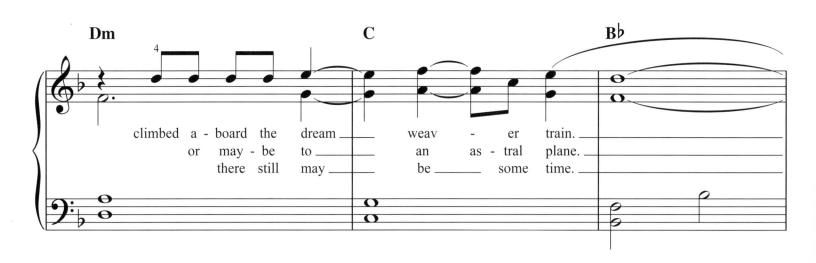

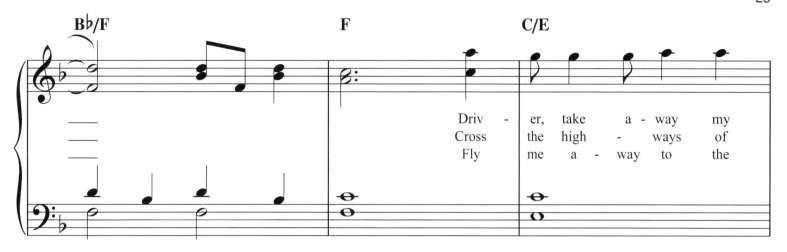

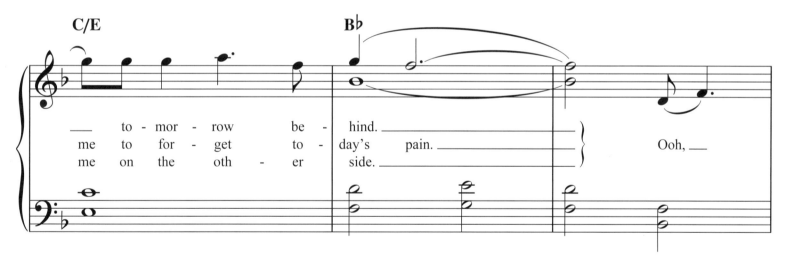

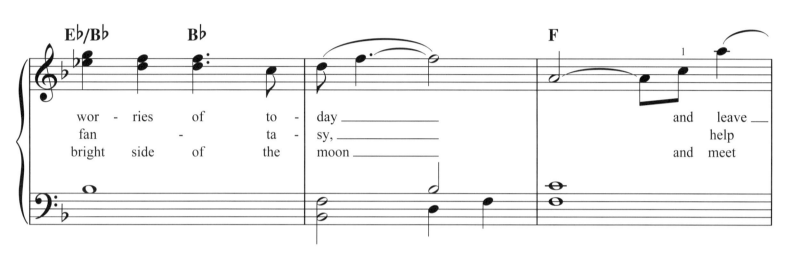

get me through _ the night. _____

Ooh, _ dream _____ weav-er,

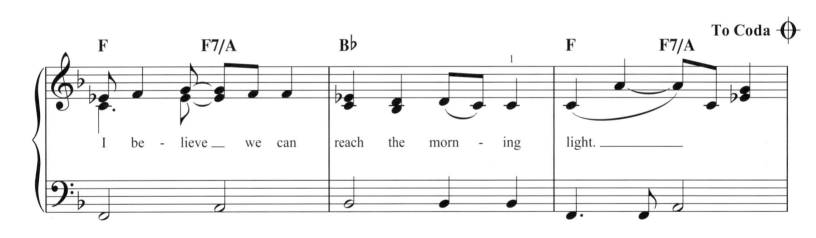

I be - lieve __ we can reach the morn - ing light. _____

To Coda ⊕

CODA ⊕

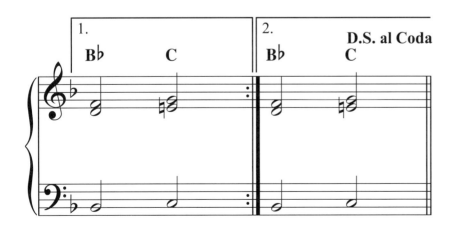

1. | Bb C

2. | Bb C D.S. al Coda

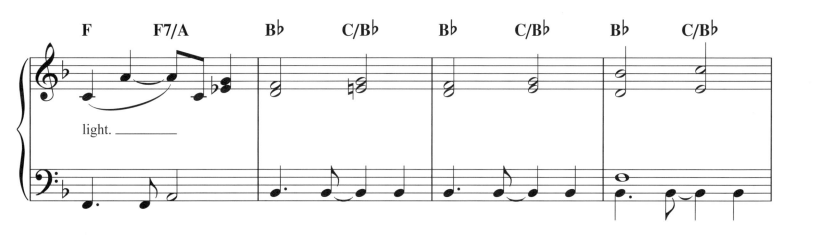

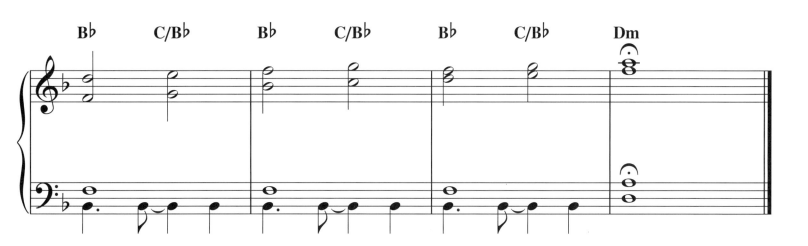

WE BELONG TOGETHER
from TOY STORY 3

Music and Lyrics by
RANDY NEWMAN

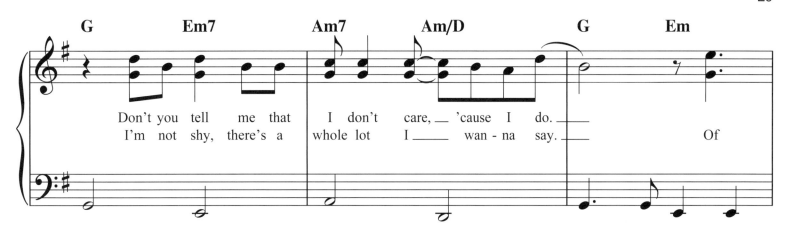

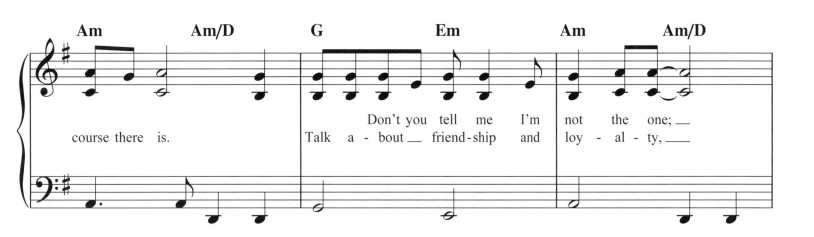

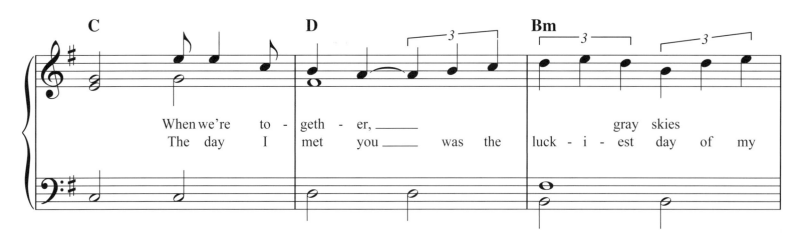

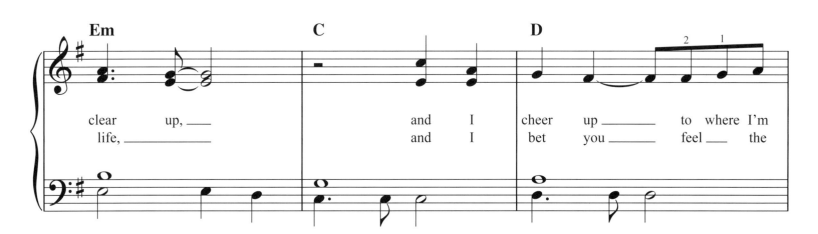

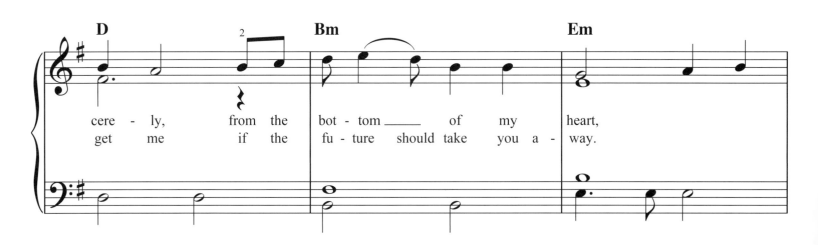

I just can't take it when we're a - part.
You know you'll al - ways be

part _____ of me.

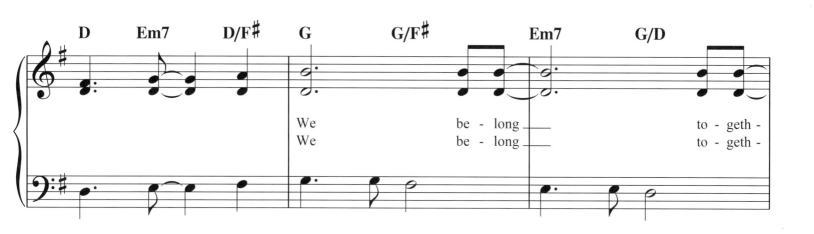

We be - long _____ to - geth -
We be - long _____ to - geth -

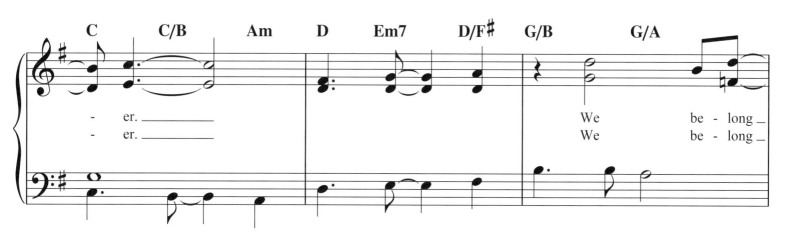

- er. _____
- er. _____

We be - long _
We be - long _

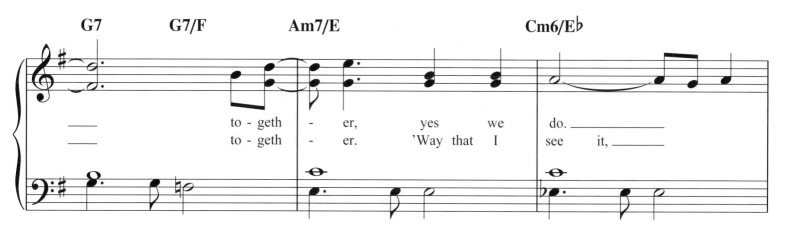

_____ to - geth - er, yes we do. _____
_____ to - geth - er. 'Way that I see it, _____

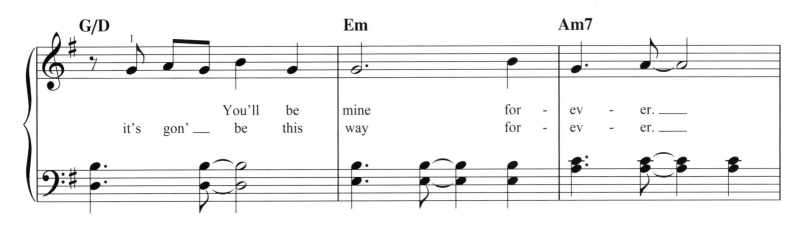

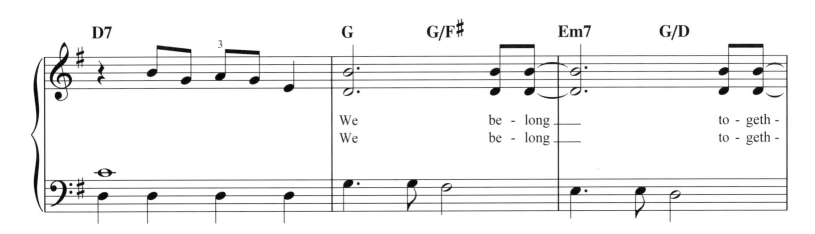

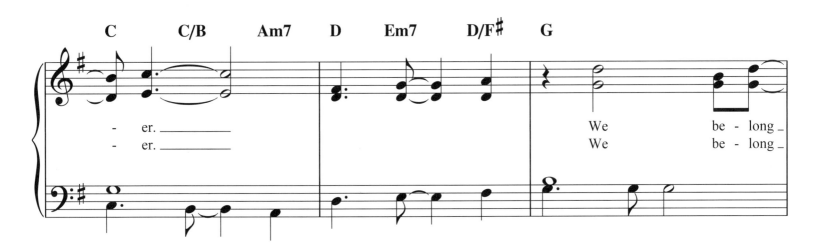

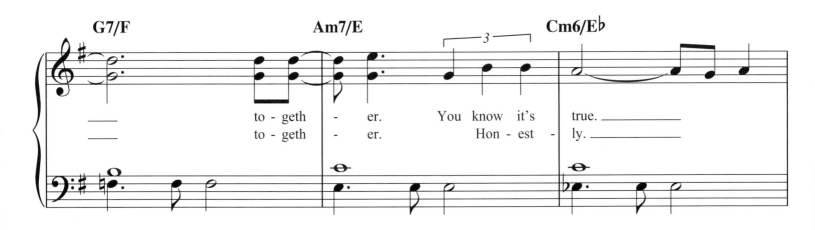

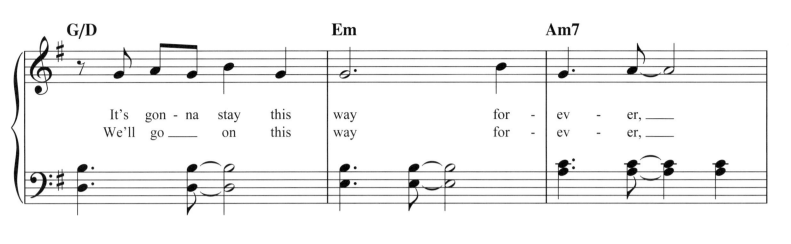

G/D   **Em**   **Am7**

It's gon - na stay this way   for - ev - er, ____
We'll go ____ on this way   for - ev - er, ____

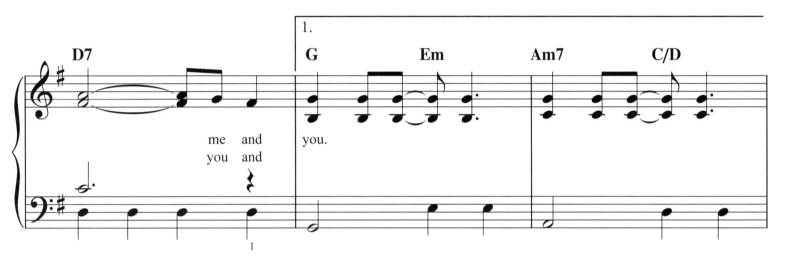

D7   1. **G**   **Em**   **Am7**   **C/D**

me and
you and   you.

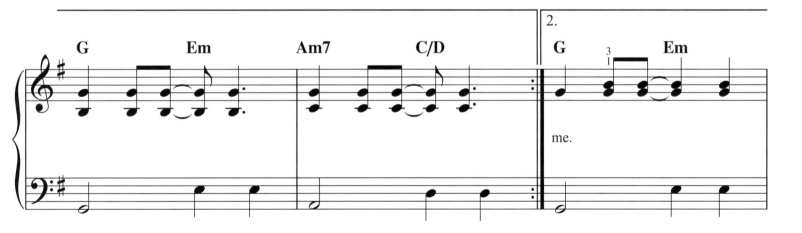

G   **Em**   **Am7**   **C/D**   2. **G**   **Em**

me.

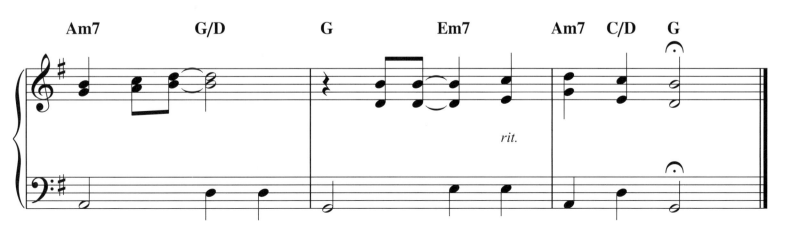

Am7   **G/D**   **G**   **Em7**   **Am7** **C/D**   **G**

rit.

YOU'VE GOT A FRIEND IN ME

(para el Buzz Español)
from TOY STORY 3

Music and Lyrics by RANDY NEWMAN
Spanish Translation by RENATO ROSENBERG

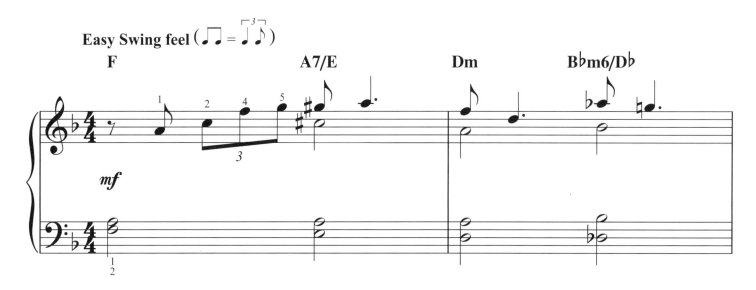

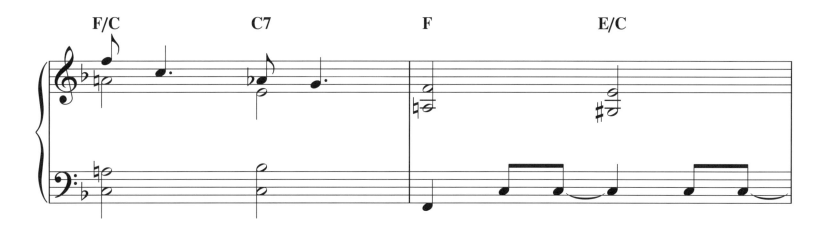

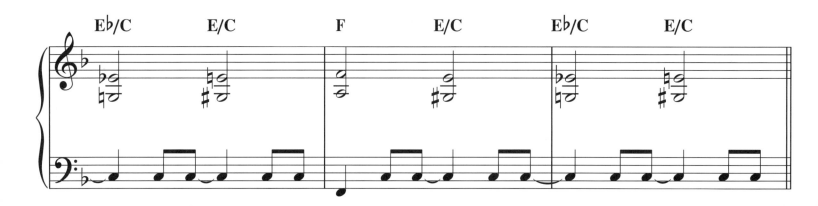

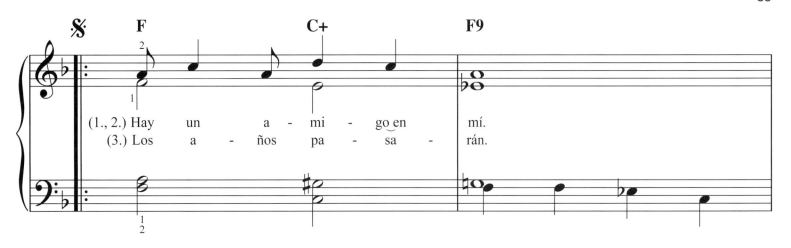

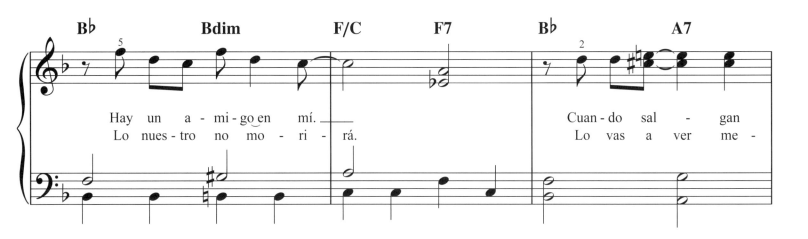

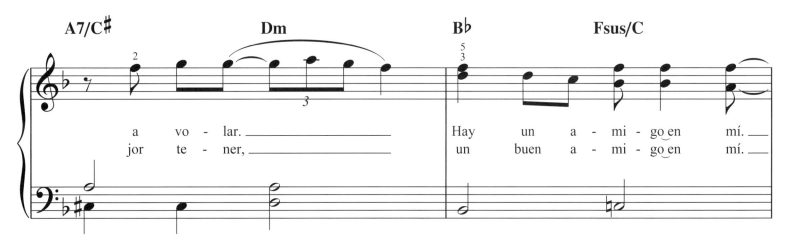

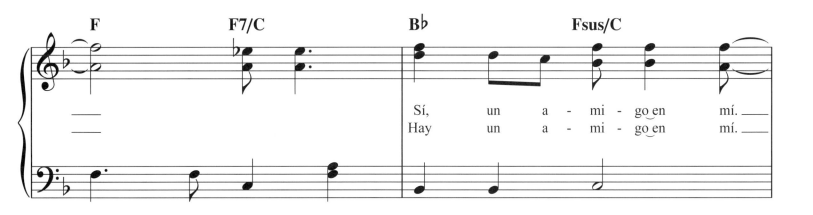

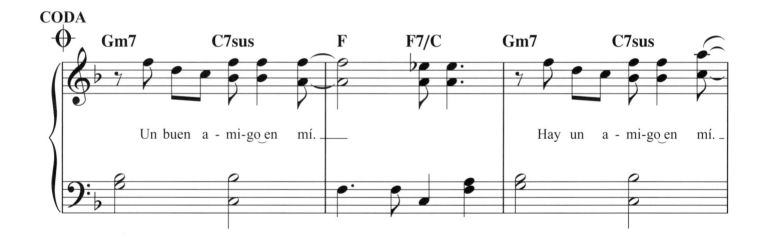

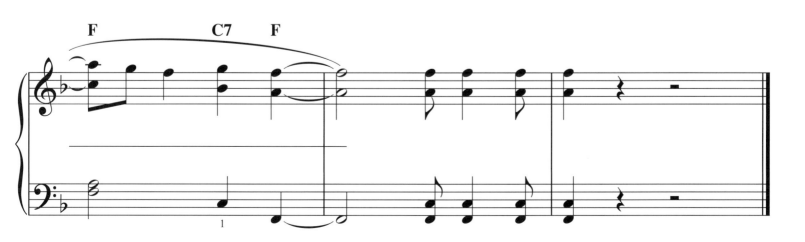

THE BALLAD OF THE
LONESOME COWBOY

from TOY STORY 4

Music and Lyrics by
RANDY NEWMAN

Moderately fast

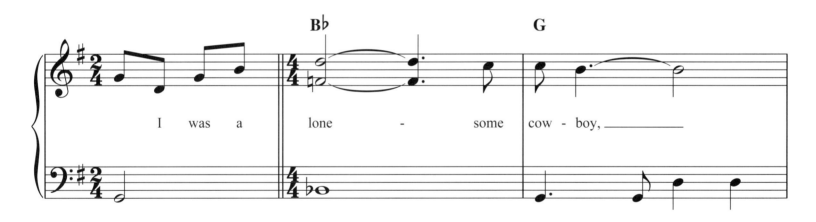

I was a lone - some cow - boy, _____

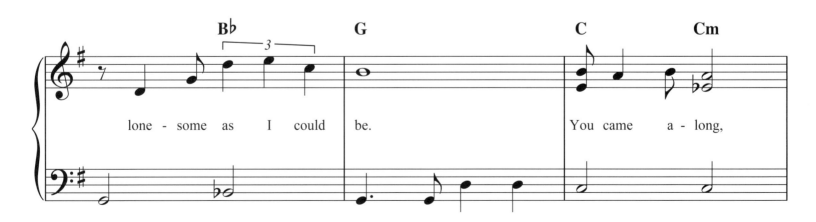

lone - some as I could be.   You came a - long,

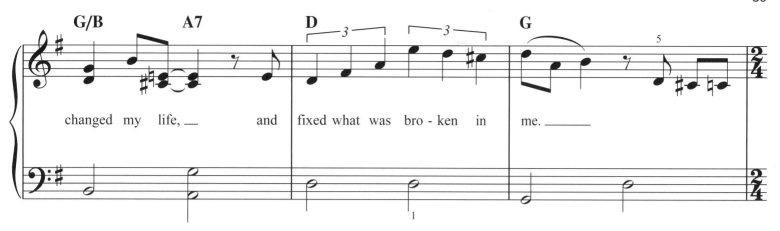

changed my life, __ and fixed what was bro - ken in me. _____

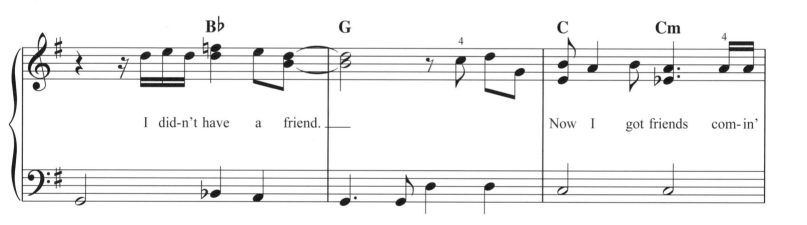

I was a lone - some cow - boy, _____

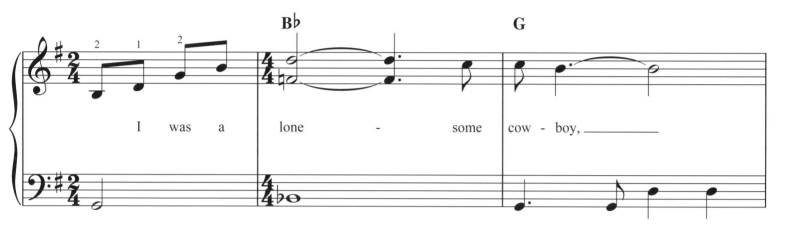

I did-n't have a friend. __ Now I got friends com-in'

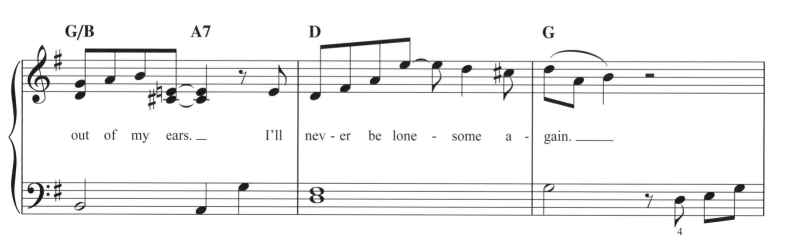

out of my ears. __ I'll nev - er be lone - some a - gain. __

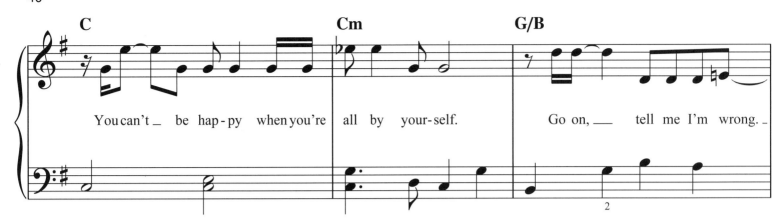

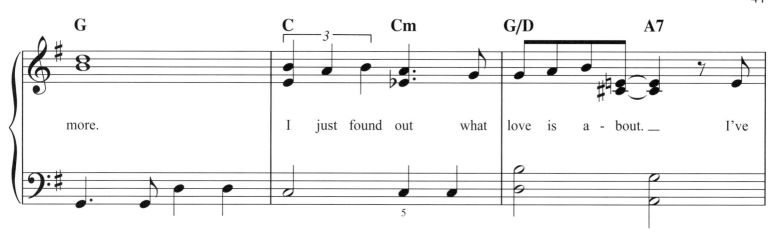

more.   I just found out what love is a - bout. ___ I've

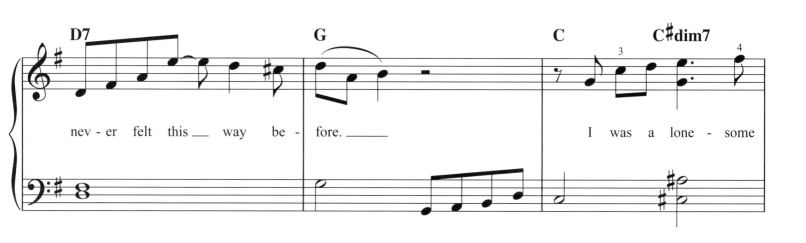

nev - er felt this ___ way be - fore. ___   I was a lone - some

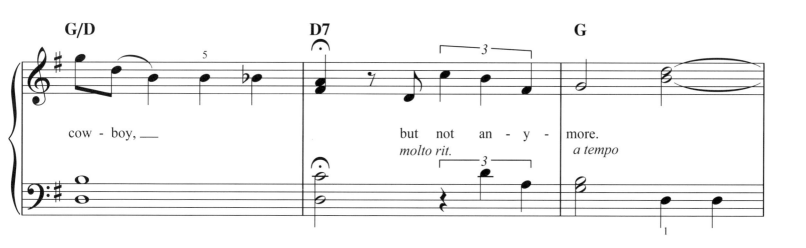

cow - boy, ___   but not an - y - more.   more.

molto rit.   *a tempo*

I CAN'T LET YOU THROW YOURSELF AWAY

from TOY STORY 4

Written by
RANDY NEWMAN

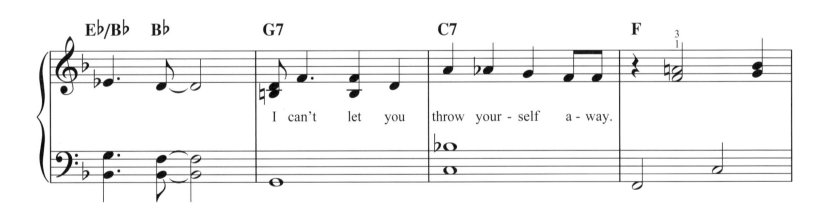

To Coda

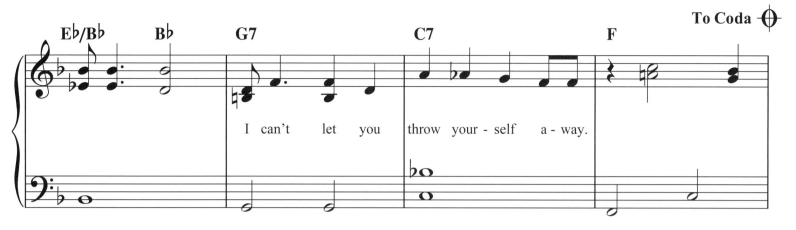

I can't let you throw your-self a-way.

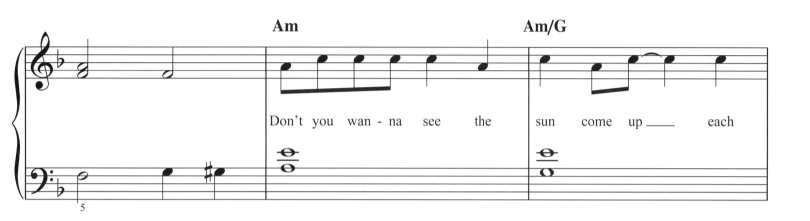

Don't you wan-na see the sun come up _____ each

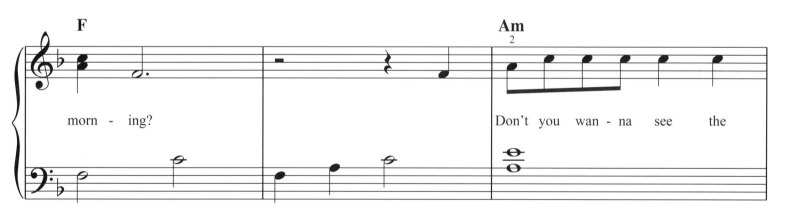

morn - ing?   Don't you wan - na see the

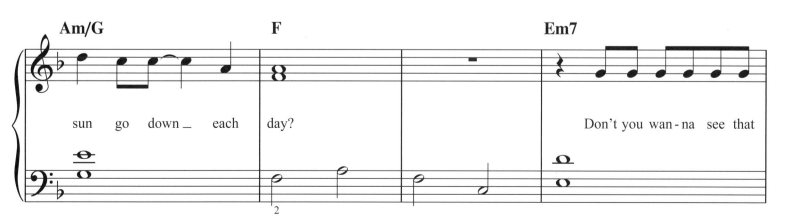

sun go down _ each day?   Don't you wan-na see that

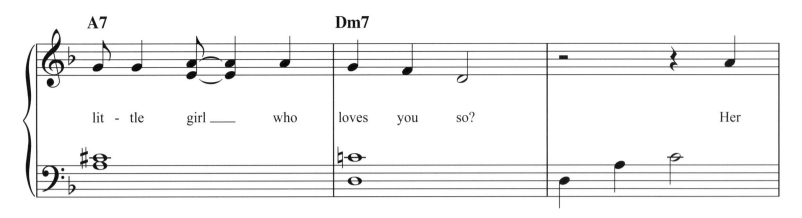

lit - tle girl ____ who loves you so? Her

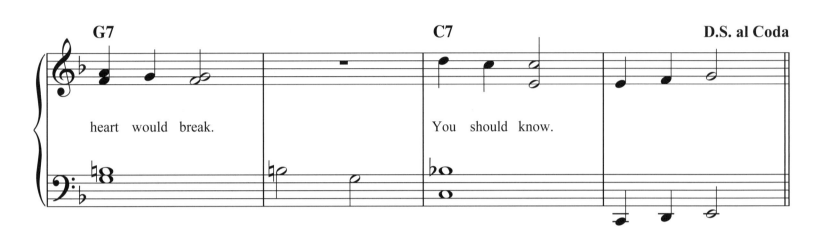

heart would break. You should know.

D.S. al Coda

CODA

Son, it seems to me like you're nev - er gon' be -

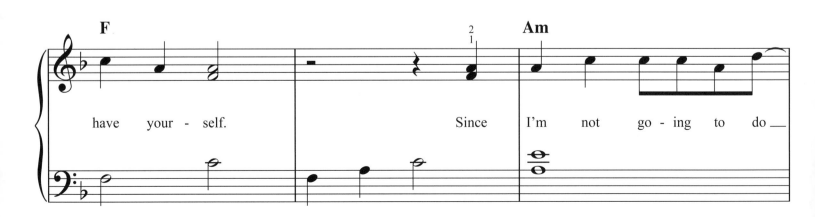

have your - self. Since I'm not go - ing to do ____

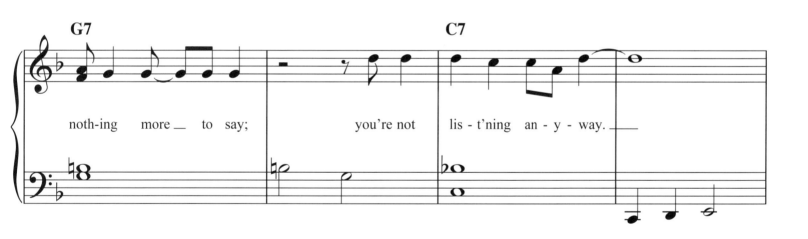

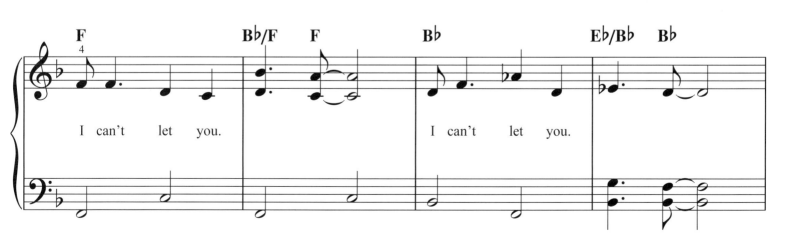

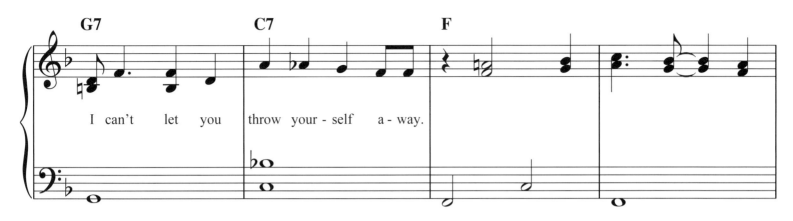

I can't let you throw your - self a - way.

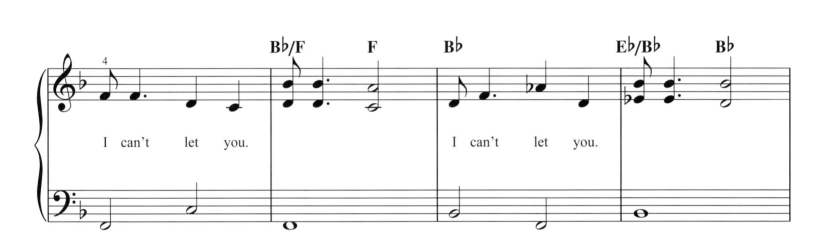

I can't let you. I can't let you.

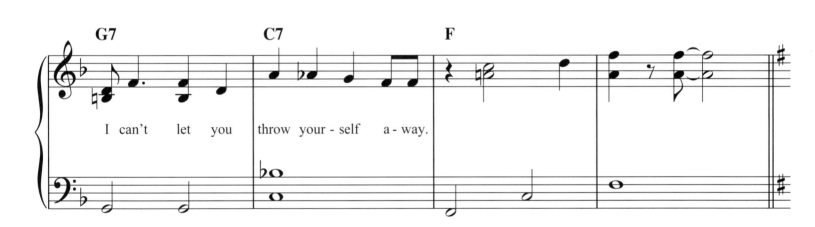

I can't let you throw your - self a - way.

I can't let you. I can't let you.

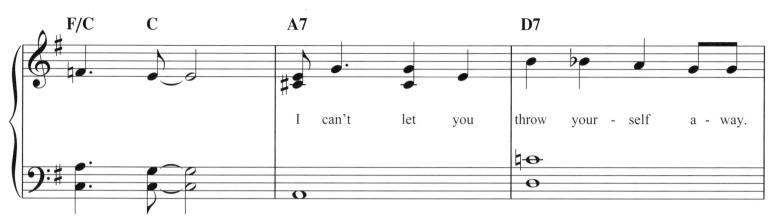

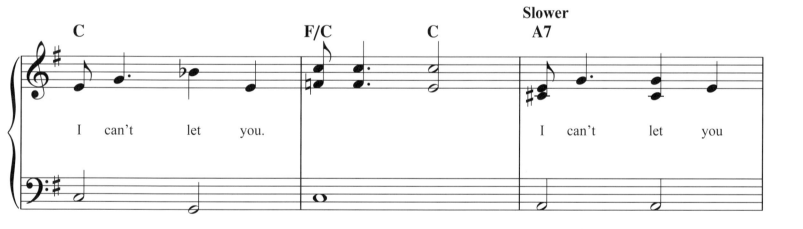

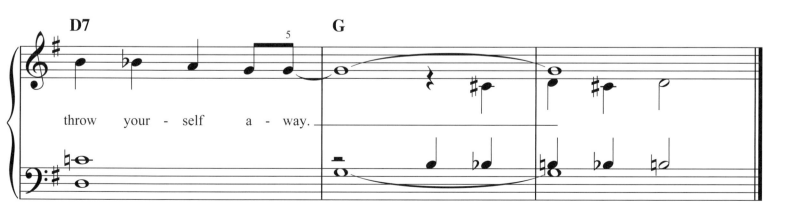